Thomas Starr King

The Organization of Liberty on the Western Continent

Thomas Starr King

The Organization of Liberty on the Western Continent

ISBN/EAN: 9783743388727

Manufactured in Europe, USA, Canada, Australia, Japa

Cover: Foto ©Suzi / pixelio.de

Manufactured and distributed by brebook publishing software
(www.brebook.com)

Thomas Starr King

The Organization of Liberty on the Western Continent

𝕿𝔥𝔢 𝔒𝔯𝔤𝔞𝔫𝔦𝔷𝔞𝔱𝔦𝔬𝔫 𝔬𝔣 𝔏𝔦𝔟𝔢𝔯𝔱𝔶 𝔬𝔫 𝔱𝔥𝔢 𝔚𝔢𝔰𝔱𝔢𝔯𝔫 𝔠𝔬𝔫𝔱𝔦𝔫𝔢𝔫𝔱.

A N

ORATION

DELIVERED BEFORE THE

MUNICIPAL AUTHORITIES

OF THE

CITY OF BOSTON,

AT THE

CELEBRATION OF THE SEVENTY-SIXTH ANNIVERSARY

OF THE

𝔇𝔢𝔠𝔩𝔞𝔯𝔞𝔱𝔦𝔬𝔫 𝔬𝔣 𝔄𝔪𝔢𝔯𝔦𝔠𝔞𝔫 𝔍𝔫𝔡𝔢𝔭𝔢𝔫𝔡𝔢𝔫𝔠𝔢,

JULY 5, 1852.

BY THOMAS STARR KING, A.M.

BOSTON:
ROCKWELL AND CHURCHILL, CITY PRINTERS.
1892.

CITY OF BOSTON.

In Board of Aldermen, December 21, 1891.

Whereas, The Fourth of July Oration delivered in 1852 by Rev. Thomas Starr King is the only one of the series since 1822 which has not been printed; and as his family is willing that it should now be issued,

Ordered, That the Chairman of the Record Commissioners, under the direction of the Committee on Printing, cause the said Oration to be printed, bound, and distributed; the edition to consist of fifteen hundred copies: and the expense, not to exceed four hundred dollars, to be charged to the appropriation for Printing.

Passed. Sent down for concurrence. December 23 came up concurred.

Approved by the Mayor December 26, 1891.

A true copy.

Attest:

John T. Priest, *Asst. City Clerk.*

PREFACE.

THOMAS STARR KING was born in the city of New York, Dec. 17, 1824, his father being the Rev. Thomas F. King, and his mother Susan Starr, both natives of that city. His father became the pastor of a church in Charlestown, where he died before his son was qualified to enter college. The young man however continued his studies while serving as a public school teacher and clerk in the Navy Yard, and in September 1846 he succeeded Rev. E. H. Chapin in the pulpit which his father had occupied. In December 1848 he married Miss Julia M. Wiggin, and soon after was installed at Hollis-street church, Boston, where he continued for eleven years. His popularity as a preacher and lecturer was very great, and few men have gained more devoted or appreciative friends.

"It was," says Dr. Henry W. Bellows, "the hidden, interior man of the heart, the invisible character behind all the rich possessions, intellectual and social, of this gifted man, that gave him his real power and skill to control the wills, and to move the hearts, and to win the unbounded confidence and affection of his fellow-beings."

In 1860, Mr. King accepted a call from a church in San Francisco. His fame as a lecturer as well as a preacher had preceded him, and he was called upon to visit all parts of our western coast. At the outbreak of the Rebellion he was thus in a position to exert a great influence upon the public of California, then tempted by the suggestion of a Pacific republic. No one who reads the pages of this

oration can doubt the energy or the eloquence with which
Mr. King combatted this heresy, nor the unflinching support which he gave to the cause of the Union. "He went
forth appealing to the people taking the constitution and
Washington for his text," and he is confessedly entitled to
the credit of having preserved the Pacific states to the
Union.

In January 1864 his new church edifice was dedicated,
but after a brief illness with diphtheria he died March 4,
1864.

Mr. King published in 1859 a well-known book in regard
to the White Hills, whose beauties were his favorite theme,
and which, in a popular sense, he almost discovered. Sev-
eral volumes of his sermons were printed after his death;
but during his life-time his compositions were reserved for
use on the lecture-platform. It was owing to this fact, that
the following Oration was not published as usual, at the date
of its delivery, by the City of Boston. Finding recently
that this was the only one in the series of Fourth of July
Orations, delivered by request of the City of Boston, which
had not been printed, application was made to the widow
and children of Mr. King, and their consent was readily
given to the publication. The manuscript was found to be
in perfect form, and only one or two verbal corrections
have been needed.

W. H. W.

CITY HALL, BOSTON, March 4, 1892.

THE ORGANIZATION OF LIBERTY ON THE WESTERN CONTINENT.

Mr. Mayor and Fellow-citizens:

The seventy-sixth anniversary of the day which proclaimed our country a distinct and independent power on the earth has dawned upon us. And it finds us in such prosperity and peace, and such rapidly increasing greatness, that our thoughts are invited to rise in adoration and gratitude to Him who "hath not dealt so with any nation," and whose favor alone is permanent strength.

The topic to which I shall ask your attention is the "Organization of Liberty on the Western Continent." In connection with this theme the Fourth of July at once assumes its real importance in our whole history, and unveils its highest claim to our reverent memory and lasting gratitude.

The day is distinguished by its historical marriage with the Declaration of Independence ; but it is not the production of that vigorous revolutionary rhetoric that we celebrate. Literature abounds with denunciations of oppressions and

assertions of human worth and rights, that have
higher quality than the periods of our venerated
state paper, and yet we do not dignify them
with national holidays. We venerate the Declaration as *a deed* more than as a composition or a
collection of doctrines. It was a bold blow for
the liberty of three millions of people; and we
should honor the noble manner in which the
deed was done, — the deliberate and solid statesmanship that comprehended the responsibilities,
and took upon its shoulders the duties of such
a radical position, — more than the words and the
deed together.

In fact, the whole Revolution itself is not of
any great importance in military history as a
series of battles and a protest of physical force.
Its achievements in the field are immortalized
by the cause it served and the manner of the
service. Our revolution was turned into a dig-
nified force instead of a flash of enthusiasm and
a rattle of musketry, by the compact, passive
resistance of character and the moral fidelity to
the cause, in privation and suffering, manifested
all over the land; through these qualities it stood
in right relations with the gravity of our earlier
history, and offered no obstructions, but powerful aid rather, to the completion of the destiny to

which from the first our land was pledged —
the peaceful organization of Liberty.

Let us glance for a moment at the physical
universe, and catch a few of the broad instructions given in it, as to the relative value of
the process of organization. Nature is not sat-
isfied with a boundless treasury of elements and
a happy balance of them into inorganic harmonies. She sends up a chorus of praise to
God as the organizer as well as creator; for her
materials are combined into forms, and the spirit
that superintends our world revels in varieties of
form that defy numeration.

The globe we live on is thoroughly organized
by an array of antagonistic forces, and is made
to play as a wheel of a celestial orrery. The
clouds, the tides, the winds, are wrapped by
laws, and made through their movement and
their oscillations to manifest subtle harmonies
that cannot be broken. Yea, even the light is
made to obey a steady rein, and to be punc-
tual as time, and exact as mathematics, in the
dispensation of its floods. The dancing light is
not suffered to be capricious and fitful in its
visitations, but is required to be dutiful, and so
that it shall break here and there in flashes, or
stream in vivid sheets now and then athwart

the darkness. Nature builds a huge home for it, stretches the immense diameter and bends the solid arches of the sun, whose gravitation poises a colony of planets, and around that rocky orb she winds the vesture of flame that is to light and warm the globes that reach from Mercury to Neptune. The steps of the vast annals of nature are marked by rising grades of organization. Each new stratum is deposited as the condition and abode of a higher animated structure; and at last the supreme skill embodied in the frame of man announces that the periods of geological development are passed.

And in history the great work is that of social organization. Providence designs that there shall be not only myriads of persons on his globe, but also civil and social structures, by which individuals shall be disposed in right relations, and many members become one body. The organization of justice, therefore, is the task which is proposed to the human race. It has steadily struggled up through the centuries towards the attainment of it; and the cheering epochs of history are those when greater advances are made and new successes permanently gained.

The student delights to retreat by his sym-

pathies into such luminous seasons of the past
as when the Greek intellect was busy in the
organization of beauty in statues, temples, eloquence, and verse; or the Egyptian genius was
throwing up from the sombre depths of its
sense of the Infinite, the Sphinx, the pyramids,
and the wild literature of future judgment and
transmigration; or when the sinews of Roman
valor and statesmanship were opening paths to
the possession of the world; or when Italy was
feeding the eyes of Europe with the rapid
wonders of her chisel and the magic of her
brush: but though less fascinating to poetic sen-
sibilities, those are the most eminent most
grand and most powerful epochs of civilization
when some great institutions loom up shaped by
the skill of many hands, beneficient in their
purpose and their agency, standing on the firm
basis of right and supporting themselves by
their own symmetry.

We shall be confirmed in this view of history
from whatever quarter we study it. Regarding
it as philosophers and watching for the advance of
truth, we shall see that no triumph of truth is so
important and so enduring as when it domesticates
itself in strong institutions and becomes entrenched in the habits of race. Regarding it

religiously, and anxious for the victory of right, we must see that there is no conquest so valuable as when justice descends into the practical life of an age, and builds its massive defences around men, investing them with rights which by general consent are considered sacred as their personality. Or if we look at history as philanthropists, still the most important and gratifying seasons will seem to be those when the welfare of men is something more than a matter of sentiment and sympathy, but is protected by the might of law and hedged by generous statutes.

The man who, by the more quiet methods of personal influence, organizes in the world a dumb institution, does vastly more than he whose radical eloquence sets the deformities of society and life in the blaze of an angry idea. The foundation of a charity school is a more memorable event than the most eloquent invective that could be preached against the selfish use of riches; a new Christian character in which religious truth is freshly embodied is a more precious contribution to the world than a new theory of holiness. History does not take account of all the hazy theories that stain the night air of time with transient radiance, any

more than the charts of Astronomy make account
of the Boreal flashes and the meteors that adorn
the winter nights with their fitful and fantastic
fire. It is only when a theory or an intellectual movement, ceasing to be a superficial
phenomenon, becomes a vital power, — a subject
not for cool geometrical measurements, but a
dynamic energy — and spreading through the intellect of genius and the sympathies of the people,
(as in the case of the principles uttered in the
Reformation, and by the first Wesleyan preach-
ers), manifests itself as a constructive force
and adds new institutions to the social land-
scape, which are vital from the core, that it
marks another hour in the advance of the race.

How easy is it to start *à priori*, and reason-
ing down from some exalted abstract principles
to condemn and scout the injustice that is
woven in with society, or by putting together
a few ideas to sketch out a perfect plan of
state, and home, and church. It is pastime for our
reveries. But to make our criticisms available;
to give our dreams a fulcrum by which they
can start rooted disorders; to make our reveries
practical and congruous with facts of human
nature, and laws of the world: we had better
try that work before we set up claims to wis-

dom. There is no more marvellous manifesta-
tion of human superiority than the ability to put
an advance political notion in practice, so that
the machine will play easily and obey the cal-
culated laws. What an expenditure of perfect
philosophies before a new and higher *fact* is
born! Humanity burns up tons of books to get
light enough for one step ahead.

Alas! gentlemen, it is not the mere existence of
steam, either in the social or the physical world,
that works wonders for humanity. It is very
easy to have steam. A little water, a match,
some charcoal, and a tea-kettle, supply all the
conditions for raising it, so that an enthusiast
may descant at leisure upon its properties, and
enjoy its prophetic and eloquent hiss. But before
the steam era in the world history begins, *the
engine* must appear out of the resources of
some practical organizing brain, and offer its
sinewy and complicated body for that intense,
vapory soul.

In the light of this analogy we say that the
peculiarity of our own history is the steady and
peaceful process of organization which it reveals,
and by which higher political truth, which the
world considered dangerous, was vindicated as
practical by being slowly clothed in fact.

Other nations have looked back to a dim antiquity for their origin. The story of their growth has been that of struggle through barbarisms and superstitions, and against wrongs and errors that were entrenched behind centuries of prescription and habit. The changes for the better have been slow, and have cost immense effort and sacrifice. Principles have dawned and then darkened, perhaps drowned, as they rise, in the red mist of war. Explosions have scattered and wasted the beneficent forces of progress; lapses of popular virtue have sunk the hopes that were justified by rising truth; and the general picture given to us is that of a feeble germ of order, striving slowly against a chaotic mass of passion, prejudice, ignorance, and wrong, by which it is often defeated, and into which up to the present time it has succeeded in throwing but few of its threads of regulated liberty.

Until the Saxon colonization of this continent, such was the stereotyped form of national experience. But with the new theatre of action prepared by Providence, a new work was imposed. There was a slow process of discovering great principles, after the foundations of our society were laid, and then a fierce contest for their first

existence on our soil. The old forces and conditions of progress with which Europe had been
acquainted, — strife of class against class for new
power or old privilege, civil war, compromise,
foreign pressure, and the shifting attitudes of
diplomacy, — have had no appreciable, certainly
no important, effect upon our progress; it has
been a rapid development of a few vigorous
convictions and principles into form. It has
been growth like that of an oak from its seed,
by gradual absorption of heat, air, and moisture,
with the occasional assistance of a storm. We
are accustomed to speak of our great struggle
as the War of *Revolution*, but strictly speaking
it was the War of *Separation* only; for it did
not bring any new organic principle into the
field of our politics, but was a resistance to the
obstructions that cramped the swelling energies of
our fundamental convictions. No one of our
constructive ideas has ever been quickened by
the angry sacrifice of blood drawn by intestine
war.

The last two centuries have been the most
remarkable of the world's history for the amount
of social justice that has been established for
millions of men; and the fullest experience of
it has been on this continent, secured by the in-

stitutions which have made our country an original
experiment and spectacle in the annals of time.
To a scientific mind, a Humboldt or an Owen,
no tidings would be freighted with such ab-
sorbing interest as the information that a new
and high type of organization had arisen on
this planet; that the creative powers around us
had given birth to some beautiful planet, some
majestic tree, some strange and symmetrical ani-
mal, with higher functions and more intricate
constitution than any vegetable or physical organization known to the lists of science. With
what reverence would their minds bend before
such a glorious miracle; and how eager, how cu-
rious and minute, would their researches be into the
wisdom embodied in this last and highest creation
of the intellect that rules the world !

We all know what excitement was caused, a
few years since, by the discovery of a new planet
beyond the path of Uranus.   But what would
the amazement of an astronomer be if he could
detect in the sky a planet in the swift process
of formation? Or what if he could look through
his glass into some sacred district of space and
see a vast continent of chaos organize itself
rapidly into an orderly system; if every process
by which planets and satellites are formed out

of primeval matter, could be made visible, and
the forces which upon our globe have so slowly
deposited the landmarks of geological ages should
condense their work into a few years, so that
he could study it at leisure, night by night,
noting each week some stage of advance which
on our globe exhausted a thousand centuries,
and seeing all ending in the production of a
beauty which our globe and our system do not
wear ? What privilege would be accounted equal
to this by an earnest, scientific mind, and how
much more clearly would the study of such a
creative process of nature reveal what the physical forces are, than any abstract description could
convey; and how much deeper and more solemn
the impression of such a spectacle than dry
statements, chemical hypotheses and mathematical
formulas !

And so our history is most interesting and
suggestive when viewed as a fresh creation from
the deeps of human nature that had long been
sluggish, and whose vitality seemed to be effete.
The appearance of our mighty millions of white
democracy, stretched from ocean to ocean and
from the Russian latitudes to the Tropical Gulf,
without a monarch, with no hereditary rulers, no
lords, no titles, no vested rights, no despotic

Church, but blest with an order such as the world
has never seen, and a prosperity that has outrun
every enthusiastic dream, and yet not exhausting
more than half a century in the revelation of
most startling results, — what is it to the political
student but a process parallel to the picture we
imagined, of an evolving system of worlds in
space before the eye of an astronomer, a magnificent and astonishing effort of organization,
unexampled in human experience for the breadth
of the scale, the rapidity of the development,
and the character of the products, and revealing
as nothing else has ever done or could do, the
constructive powers that slumber in the popular
brain and heart.

Many of the facts of our history in which
the Old World was concerned, catch a provi-
dential hue, when seen, from the principle that
this continent was wanted for new organizations
of society. We see a pregnant coincidence in
the fact that the colonization did not begin till
after the Protestant reformation had established
itself, and that the Spaniards found no motives
to claim and people the northern seaboard. A
light is thrown upon the strenuous struggle of
England and France in relation to a portion of
our territory; the great expenditure of blood

and treasure; and the skilful diplomacy which drove the French from the valley of the Ohio, — thus preparing the way for the consolidation of the American colonies, — giving them a friend in the government of France, while it banished from the great Western domains a race too much incumbered with the traditions of the past and too feeble in the faculties of organization to be worthy or able to dot that fresh country with new forms of government and society. Especially we are called to study reverently the process by which the Protestant world was first sifted and winnowed, till the choicest germs of character were found strong enough to send out the shoots of lasting institutions on a hard soil and under a hostile sky.

Nothing strikes the student with more force, as he looks back over the rise of our republic, than the small proportion of published or meditated theorizing about the rights of man, the province of government, and the destiny of our race, compared with the actual results that are visible. We have already intimated that there are two great classes of men related to the world's progress. One class are fine critics of social disorder and injustice in the light of favorite ideas. They are accurate analysts; perhaps they are able to make outlines and draughts of a polity or society that would exclude most of the evils that oppress mankind; but they have no force in the world. They cannot interest men in their plans, and the moment they come in contact with the real forces of society and human nature they and their theories are powerless as babes. All their energy runs to the brain and expends itself through the voice and the proportions of a theory.

If the world were made of paper, if ink were the life-blood of the universe, and things were no deeper than a mathematician's diagram, they would be the hope and salvation of the race. But the world is made up of something quite different from paper; and so we may rejoice that there is another class of men who have far less skill in theories, but far greater constructive capacity in the world of facts, men of influence, men who, wherever you place them, become centres of force, and soon dispose men and circumstances into an order where they move with more harmony and efficiency. Compared with the class first named, these last are as the seed of a tree in contrast with a clear description of it, or the chemical formulas of what its substance is. To use a sentence of Carlyle, "there is in them what transcends all logic utterance, a congruity with the unuttered." They live, and, "institutions are their lengthened shadows." Need I say that the men who first colonized the Plymouth sands and the shores of Boston bay were of the latter stamp. They had not spent much time in reveries about liberty as an ideal goddess. They came to labor as soon as they stepped upon the soil, with the undertone of conviction that freedom, as a working power, — a Hercules rather than an Apollo, a hero of toil, more than a patron of theories and dreams, — was to use them as the first channels through which its creative energy could pour itself into new forms for the benefit of many generations.

The men who stepped upon the bleak shores of New England had been so trained by hardship and oppression that every free sentiment their breasts harbored was as stubborn as their ribs, and every idea of rights which their heads supported had roots that were twisted in the sub-soil of their being. The strength of their faith in liberty could not be expressed in declamation or treatise; wherever they lived the effluence of their characters would have purified the social air, and their daily work have assisted the establishment of social righteousness.

Let us imagine an intelligent man, wholly ignorant of our earliest annals, but aware that the institutions and power of this country are the products of the last two centuries, beginning an examination of the primitive records of the New England settlements. Would he not expect to find some clearly outlined scheme of a great State and a Briarean government? Would he not confidently search for the sketch of a civil constitution and a theory of political equality and balances which the colonists determined that the forests should make way for, and the wise labor of their posterity strengthen and extend? How surprised would he be to discover that there were no such schemes; that the vessels that discharged the colonists were disburthened of no such theories! Or rather, the theories were *in the blood* of the men themselves.

What they sought and determined to gain was a few fundamental rights that would hedge their manhood and their faith. They wanted a simple, social structure, humble as their log-huts and Puritan chapels, that would house a prosperous and pious community and a peaceful brotherhood. They were not furious for the aggressive establishment of a social philosophy; their vitality had not been expended brain-wards in shaping and perfecting the ideal proportions of a pet theory. They had no more decided the minutiæ of their policy than they had decided on what spot they would put their dwellings; and so they had the immense advantage of grappling directly with circumstances by the working passions of men and the strong forces of their common sense, from which, in its purification by suffering, the crusts of feudal prejudice had dropped.

How much better for humanity that a Carver, a Winthrop, or a Brewster, were landed here with their circles of friends, than that the partisans of some Plato's "Republic," or Harrington's "Oceana," or Owen's "Harmony," had been disembarked! Each one of the men who were sent by Providence was a vitalized treatise, a seed corn of better societies and new ages. They came to build the institutions of the future, not by copying from any comprehensive, sharp-lined, radical vision, but by discharging into their first work a flood of rough vitality that could not but swell beyond its rind and gather larger structures for its home. They labored for the future and undreamed America as the beavers understand masonry and statics; and like the bees, the tiny Paxtons of entomology, whose geometry is not learned from Euclid but pervades their substance.

They had, too, the balance of powers that is necessary to every vigorous and lasting structure of society. They were bold, very bold, but not too bold. No set of men, however logical their protests against false habits and base laws, however clear their perceptions of truthful principles, can put much vital force into a new constructive movement if they are not consecrated and loyal men; if, in the centre of their being, they do not account themselves as subjects and instruments, and look toward some quarter of the Infinite with the shaded gaze of worship. In our ancestors, their faith, their courage, and the licentious iconoclasm to which the fresh forests might have invited their sense of wrong, were steadied and corrected by their reverence. They were not so out of patience with the past and with the land that had wronged them, that they could not appreciate its real wisdom, and be content to use what had worked well in their own country's experience. Repelled by the bitter experience of persecution from many of the ideas and social principles which were inwoven with the structure of society in the Old World, their minds swung with the centrifugal force of a planet towards a new order; and yet were bolted, by an energy firm and still as the centripetal rein, to a regular track.

It is fortunate that they did not come here with any schemes based on a dissection of human nature, and strive to anticipate centuries, if not to wrestle against the truth, by building a social fabric on the results of a shadowy analysis. They had not, like Fourier and his disciples, made any scientific inventory of the possible constructive powers of our nature, which they were eager to reflect in a community. If they had, the aboriginal communities in the American forests of wild cats, partridges and raccoons, would have received little detriment from a spreading civilization.

Instead of such an aim they affirmed the responsibilities of authorities. They had constructed no schemes of "hypominor" groups and "hyperminor" series in a perfect society, nor of "passional dominants" and "passional tonics," nor of the low accords and the cardinal accords of friendship, nor of the relative rank of ambition, love, and "familism" as forces in the state; but they struck for the intervention of the people in public affairs. They had not speculated finally about the precise ties that should connect the individual and the state, but they looked out for personal liberty, and they guaranteed trial by jury. The scheme of a phalanstery, in which children should be swung in a community of cradles, and trained from their "initial crisis" to their "citerior transition," (that is, from the moment when the baby gown is wanted to the time when the jacket shows symptoms of development), had never entered their heads; but they knew how to make the home sacred with the spirit of piety, and to startle nature with the humble architecture of the public school. No visions of landscapes laid out in geometrical order and proportioned nicely to the tastes of the cultivators had woven themselves out of the gossamer tissue into which truth may be unravelled by a diseased analysis, but they provided that roads should be built, and that land should not be prevented from partition by laws of primogeniture. They could not have conceived such finespun harmonies of structure in an ideal state as Plato outlined and St. Simon meditated, but they knew how to fix the running gear of a social order that should give a larger degree of homely justice than the world had imagined possible; they knew how to give beneficent power to grand juries, constables, and judges; how to appoint registrars, clerks, and surveyors;

how to hedge the town-meeting with solemn
forms, and to keep a determined eye on the
Habeas Corpus. Coming out of ages of feudal-
ism and despotism, they had the sturdy sense
"to ordain the maximum of administration and
the minimum of government," "to keep power
as much as possible in the hands of those most
disposed to suffer from its abuses;" and to place
the conservative element, (as Mr. Hillard has so
wisely and so happily said,) "not in the limita-
tion of political rights, but in the multiplication
of political trusts."

The founders of our land organized the American township, the grandest practical movement
of the human intellect hitherto made in society,
since it reversed the old methods by which political existence and civil rights had been slowly
communicated from the superior classes downward,
and affirmed them for the whole people, and
guarded each man's possession of them by the
magic ring of law. This was the archetypal
leaf which contained the secret of the structure
of the plant, the primitive cell which throughout
nature is the nucleus from which the highest
organisms start, and by the multiplication of
which they are easily formed. So great was the
genius shown in the structure of these town-

ships, and so vast and far-reaching their importance, that De Tocqueville's eulogy is justified, — "The boldest theories of the human reason were put into practice by a community so humble that no statesman condescended to attend to it; and a legislation without precedent was produced off-hand by the imagination of the citizens."

From the township the county was developed, and gradually the lineaments of an organized colony began to show themselves through the practical application of the idea of representative government, which another French writer of our century has called "one of the few great discoveries that among the moderns has created a new universe." From the earliest times and in every colony there seems to have been something in the air and soil of America to foster the idea of representative power as a first principle of American thought. We should all be acquainted with the quaint phrases in which an old historian informs us concerning Virginia, that, "In 1620 a house of burgesses broke out in the Colony." Such an eruption shows us what was the quality of the popular blood. What does it teach us but that the flushes of indignation at threatened oppression in the first settlements were not destructive but creative movements, opening legal and orderly channels for their vent? What was this strange eruption but the blush of American expression upon the infant countenance of the body politic, which was to be confirmed and stamped into it as a characteristic in coming years? The same historian writes, too, that in Massachusetts, "although there is no color for it in the Charter, a House of Deputies suddenly appeared in 1634, to the surprise of the Magistrates and the disappointment of their scheme for power." Whence could such a beneficient apparition have started but from the deeps of the American passion for freedom, which has proved itself wiser than all the schemes of studious critics of liberty, and which thus far has known how to meet every emergency from the resources of its organizing common sense?

There is something quite amusing in the tone with which Massachusetts met the proposition of friendly Lords in England to grant them and their families hereditary honors, if they should remove to this land. The proposition was not met by any clear argument against the injustice of it, or its discordance with their plans of society; it was rebutted by an odd expression of reverence which showed more convincingly than the most forcible logic could, how

hopeless was the prospect of transplanting such
honors into American respect; — "When God
blesseth any branch of any noble or generous
family with a spirit and gifts fit for government,
it would be a taking of God's name in vain to
put such a talent under a bushel, and a sin
against the honor of magistracy to neglect such
in our public elections. But if God should not
delight to furnish some of their posterity with
gifts fit for magistracy, we should expose them
and the Commonwealth to reproach and prejudice, if we should call them forth, when God
doeth not, to public authority." A fresh, cool
blast of political truth setting back upon the
sickly air of Europe from the pious democracy
of the wilderness !

Various as were the forms of colonial constitution in America, and however contrary the
claim might be to the letter and spirit of the
charters, representative government was insisted
on as a fundamental necessity, indispensable to the
control of their own interests and the security
of future freedom. Struck to the earth by the
oppressions of the Old World, the Saxon Antæus
rose up from contact with the aboriginal soil,
surcharged with this instinct of representative
rights, which was yet to prove fatal to his foe.

Rhode Island attained and kept it; Connecticut organized it; Virginia, as we have seen, grasped it, and would not let it go; New York clung to it with vigor: and the struggle through which the Carolinas insisted on and secured it showed that it must be an organizing principle of the continent.

Nothing, indeed, can illustrate more brilliantly the difference between a theoretical legislation, however symmetrical its proportions, and that which has the vital spirit of a people in it and therefore is good for them because it fits them, than the reception given by the people of Carolina to the constitution drafted for them by Shaftesbury the statesman and Locke the philosopher. Viewed as a play of some of the best European notions of liberty into pure space, a leisurely exercise in political mathematics by reflective men immured in their libraries, it was no doubt a pleasant exercise to draw its outline; and if it had been applied to men without passions, a colony of human puppets, no doubt the machinery would have run without much friction. In the study of a philosophical lord what could be finer and more symmetrical than the division of Carolina into equal counties, with an Earl and two Barons for each, to whom a large portion of the land was forever deeded; the elective franchise conferred on freeholders of fifty acres; an aristocratic court to superintend the press: and a Parliament to which only large land-holders were eligible. But the social diagrams and the titles that looked so fine on English parchment could not be repeated in American fact. The soil would not support a Landgrave; the counties refused hospitality in their landscapes to a Baron's palace and estate: and the people found that they could not work at all in the artistic vestures of law which philosophy had cut and stitched for them. They resisted the blessing upon which so much philosophic ink and oil had been expended, and it was not many years before the model which, in England, as we read, " was esteemed by all judicious persons without compare," but under which the Carolinas had not known one day of real enjoyment, was forever abandoned, and the inhabitants trusted to their own wisdom and the organic power of their own sense of justice, as superior to all that scientific and foreign skill could accomplish in their behalf.

It was of great importance to the nobility and success of our revolution that there had

been this steady, organizing force in the country
from its earliest date. For it gave body to that
struggle; it enabled the people to comprehend it
from the first; it gave them something to grasp
as an object for which to sacrifice, and to have
a steady passion and a systematic enthusiasm
for: and thus their devotion was saved from
souring into a mad idea of popular discontent,
suspicion, and ferocity, as all long contentions
for embodied principles are sure at last to do.
It is fortunate for us that it was not the rights
of *man*, but the rights of *men*, that the Revolution affirmed and defended. In the felicitous
language of the orator * whose admirable production adorned this occasion two years ago,
'the people fought for ideas that were facts and
liberties that were laws.'

The next great step in the process of organization was through the blood, the storm, and
the sacrifice of the Revolution, by which the
colonies, achieving independence, rose to be
American States. He who would know the
glory of the struggle which this day commemo-
rates, must study the quickening influence it
exerted upon the republican principle in the land,
so that it suddenly sprung into higher and
vigorous forms. In most of the colonies, what-

---

* Edwin P. Whipple's Oration, p. 8, line 5.

ever aristocratic and feudal elements and preju-
dices lingered in the public mind, speedily
disappeared during the progress of the struggle
or at its close. The Tories were the scape-
goats that bore away into banishment all the
sentiment of that character that might lead the
communities into public sin. The very statute
books shook themselves free of all legislation
that interfered with popular supremacy. It was
not through violent disruptions and earth-
quake throes of society, but peacefully, that our
Democracy rose to its lasting empire. Even
those whose interests were invaded by it offered
no obstacles, when the revolution was over, to
the full organizing sweep of the dominant idea.
Its battle-grounds were conventions; its contests
were speeches; its weapons were votes; its
victories were laws: and public prosperity is the
constant ovation it receives.

What a feature of our history is this, that all
the experience and all the laws of society on the
other continent have been contradicted and over-
ridden in our growth; and while not a single privilege or right of the people in other countries has
been gained at less expense than violent shocks
and agitations, and the shedding of rivers of blood,
here the germ of liberty planted on a thin and

frozen soil, has run through its upward stages
without let or hinderance from ourselves, by the
forth-putting power of its own life, revealing the
gradual progress of its theory by some new
shoot of institution or statute and showing in
our history, through a process slightly less peaceful than the growing harvest, "first the blade,
then the ear, after that the full corn in the
ear." *Sans Culotte-ism,* as Carlyle describes it,
came up into French society, like a fiend from
the pit, snorting fire, and screaming to the
terror-smitten nation "What will you do with
me?" But from the ocean deeps of our history,
through the blood-stained foam of the Revolution, rose the Republican Aphrodite, perfect in
her proportions, blessing the day with a peaceful smile, whose presence the land she stepped
upon rejoiced in, yielding the green herbs to
her soft and delicate tread.

And now our attention must be given to
the last and crowning stage of organization.
The idea of a union among the colonies had
floated through the popular mind, and it was
gradually shaping itself into distinctness for
years. There was the dim but deepening feel-
ing, inspired by Providence, that the work of
organization to which this continent was dedi-

cated, would not be fulfilled till a central structure rose, that should represent the power and
harmonize the interests of the lesser republics
that were clustered on the soil. It was proph-
esied by the early union among the colonies of
New England. Faint suggestions of the necessity of it were fostered by the growing oppressions of the parent land, making the colonies
thrill with a common vexation and a common
consciousness of wrong. A conception of it
engaged the practical and patriotic brain of
Franklin, and at one time was favorably viewed
even in England. The peril of liberty in the
years preceding the revolutionary outbreak acted
as a consolidating pressure.

The general interests and passions, during the
war, found a representative focus in the hall of the
Continental Congress. In the confederation that
succeeded, a stanch and legal bond was sought, for
amity and power; but it was not wisely enough constructed to unify interests, and sectional passions
and jealousies soon made ominous breaches in it.
War was over; peace had come; but where was
the one America that should have stood out shapely
and strong, after the storm had blown away?
The temple of western liberty was yet *unroofed*.
The rock had been laid bare for its corner-

stones; its foundations had been laid by a glorious company of workmen whose masonry needed no repair; its majestic columns had been raised in such stately strength, and with such various ornament, that the love of beauty and power in those who gazed upon them found little that was lacking; its peaceful enclosures were filled with thousands and hundreds of thousands whose fathers had laid the stubborn base and built the floors, and whose own genius and valor had lifted the pillars and carried up the walls.

But the covering of the vast edifice had baffled the skill of the architects. The Articles of Confederation were but an unsightly tent which the winds and the rain soon stripped into ribbons, leaving the multitudes unhoused under the fierce sunlight, the night skies, and the storm. Shall the constructive genius of the land prove unequal to this culminating problem? Has the victorious war imposed a duty which the conquerors cannot meet? Is the spectacle of shattered Germany and fragmentary Italy to be repeated in the unconstellated and hostile lights of the western firmament? and must the promise of our history and the pointings of Providence, and the hope of every preceding struggle, be fruitless, and the expectation of the world be

denied its satisfaction ? No, the intellect of the
land is equal to the most difficult scheme of
organization. For the great builders have gone
aloft to consider the plans of a fitting super-
structure. *He* is at their head whose sword
bore no terror to the liberty which his military
genius saved from foreign injury, and whose
organizing character lifts the name of *Washington*
higher than the fellowship of camps to the
selectest list of statesmen. And now the mighty
rafters of the Constitution rise, to be stretched
from pillar to pillar across the walls; and see!
the immense and glorious dome of the national
government arches over the space below, to give
shelter to the thronged and joyous multitudes,
and from the staff that crowns it streams the
banner of the One Republic, the last and great-
est creation of a race in history.

Let it be our prayer that the dome thus raised
may cover and crown the edifice for ages, that the
flag which streams from its summit, stained though
it is with many spots, shall float there, that the
winds and the storms of public sentiment may
wash it clean; knowing that the edifice is incom-
plete and weak without its coping and its roof, and
that if the summit fall, it must be to the ruin of
the walls and the burial of thousands by its crash.

Within our own generation the capacity of our country for the organization of liberty has made itself brilliantly manifest, and has won many triumphs. We have become so accustomed to the facts that we are not startled by the marvel which the facts reveal; but if we could look at it with fresh eyes and in the light of any other history than our own, we should see that our western colonization and the institutions that have kept pace with it, are so surprising that they might almost be accounted miraculous. When we see those mighty living tides of English, German, Irish, and Scandinavian emigration flowing westward and crystallizing as they flow into beautiful social order, where shall we turn to find anything in history by which it can be paralleled or even understood ? What is there in annals of time that will compare with the joyous song of humanity as it marches through the forests and valleys of the West, cutting the timber that obstructs its way into school-houses and churches, sweeping back the wolf and the deer, the buffalo and the bear, that instead of their howl and tramp, the air may be stirred with the eloquence of the caucus and the music of the choir, bidding the wild torrents and the fresh vapors hiss, and the implements of cunning labor fly, in compacting a civilization that combines freedom, culture, and religion, until the spirit that stepped upon the Plymouth sands is greeted by his grandchild at the Rocky Mountains and the free charter of California, — God save it from the disgrace of ever being other than free! — emblazons in the sight of China the principles caught from Faneuil Hall.

The human race has never, before this experience of the West, had the opportunity to show what results, in the way of organization, it could work if left alone.

One branch of the Christian Church in Europe throws its influence for the forces of despotism, on the ground that the human race itself is not equal to the production and maintenance of a new and beneficient institution. It affirms that the uninspired intellect of man is essentially anarchical, and that God has fixed by his own wisdom the forms of the family, the nobility, the throne, and the church, as the safeguards of all the peace that is possible; beyond which, if the irreverent ambition of man would stray, it ordains confusions and sins against Heaven. There is something sublime in the positive audacity of this theory, and humanity pleads against it with a rhetoric equally sublime. She brings deep lat-

itudes and wide longitudes of liberty to answer
it; she points to Cincinnati and Indianapolis, to
a country between Lake Huron and Lake Michi-
gan, to Wisconsin and Iowa, to the institutions
that look down into the Pacific from the head-
lands of the Golden State and the Oregon,
which have grown up without noise into order and
prosperity, during the lifetime of the generations
that have made Europe restless with throes for
liberty, and while the logic has been promul-
gated which defames the popular power. Will
it be said by the partisans of the theory in
question that Providence has inspired the Ameri-
cans for this work? Then Providence does not
patronize despotism in the nineteenth century;
and if our western countrymen have had no aid
of inspiration, then the theory falls, for new
institutions can grow out of, and rest upon, the
popular mind.

On the continent of Europe, there is at
this moment no political organization of men.
They are agglomerated by force. They are
heaped and crowded into tyrannical conditions, where their loves, reverences, and ideas
will not suffer them to combine; government there
bears the same relation to an organization that
clay packed into a mould bears to a crystal.

The elements of modern civilization have always been jumbled there, and every effort which they have made of late for proper development and harmonious reconstruction has been met by lines of bayonets and blaze of cannon. It is well, therefore, that against the philosophy which supports the despots of the eastern world there should have arisen in our own day the magnificent refutation of the West; that the depths of our forests and the sweep of our prairies, should have answered the frown of St. Petersburg and the taunt of the Vatican, by a civilization whose rise is spotted with no drop of blood, and whose proportions show that the genius of our race, unhampered by despots, does know how to organize liberty in solid fact and vigorous law.

As we speak of the West, the subject itself, no less than our instinctive sympathy and sorrow, dictates an expression of respect and veneration for the memory of the statesman and the orator, whose worn frame, — the silent shrine of a rare, electric soul — will soon be laid for perpetual rest in that beloved soil. When his eyes first saw the light, the wilderness was scarcely broken, which, rapidly filling with hardy settlers, he helped in his early manhood to cover with American laws, and which, as a rising

State, he represented in the national councils, and glorified by his patriotism, his eloquence, his statesmanship, and a power of personal influence rarely equalled, and never, probably, surpassed.

" From the charmed council to the festive board,
   Of human feelings the unbounded lord;
   In whose acclaim the loftiest voices vied,
   The praised — the proud — who made his praise their pride."

The business of eulogy is not for me or for this time. But the workings of American institutions can hardly find clearer and more brilliant illustration than in the fact that he, the great commoner, the Chatham of the Republic, was the child of poverty and the builder of his own greatness, rising early by the force of genius to a sway of men, more powerful than any titled autocrat can claim; and leaving such a vacancy as he sinks into his grave, that for thousands and hundreds of thousands in our land, the joy of this jubilee is dimmed by the thought that its dawning light and mid-day splendor fall upon the pale brow, the pulseless heart, the unnerved hand, and death-locked lips of HENRY CLAY.*

---

* Henry Clay was born in Hanover County, Va., 12 April, 1777, and died in Washington, D.C., 29 June, 1852.

Thus it has been the great distinction of our country that it has been the home of a more marvellous building capacity than any other land can show. Without having given to the world a single new work of much value to illumine the dark regions of social science, it has peopled a continent with institutions of which the projection in literature would have been denounced by lovers of order as a licentious and destructive dream. Nay, even for the best works that analyze and illustrate our own institutions, the American student is compelled to look abroad.

We are often stigmatized as a boasting people, too subject to gusts of extravagant impulses, too fond of exaggerated rhetoric, too much in love of showy and flattering words, and therefore at the mercy of the loose-tongued demagogue. We know on what aspects of society these charges are founded, but where is the people that in proportion to its talk has done so much that time will not attack ? But may we not claim it as a glorious distinction of our people, that though they are more than patient of florid rhetoric in the caucus and on the stump, they have always been distrustful of it in the Senate Chamber ? that they have always been wary of organizing declamation or flighty theory into a code ? and that, so far as the attitude of the state towards new measures and other countries is concerned, it has been determined, not by whirlwinds of sentiment, but by cool reflection and sharp debates ?

We may proudly hold it up as the peculiarity of our republic, that the people revere still the stiff speech of a statute more than they delight in frothy garrulities of fancy; and that before the plan of a demagogue can claim the sanction of those solemn words "be it enacted," it must pass through more refining processes than the heat of a caucus, and be hammered by some discussion that is solid with common sense. The men who hold the pens that write our statutes are generally organizers rather than dreamers and declaimers; and there is no more striking characteristic of our society than the fact that the gusty breath of a continental democracy has imparted so little instability and fluctuation to the laws.

The instructions which these thoughts furnish are simple and obvious. First, gratitude to the Providence that decreed this soil to men whose experiments for liberty were guided by a constructive instinct and a courageous prudence, rather than to men of more daring speculation and feebler hands. Who cannot see how much more has been done for liberty beyond our shores, by the slow and solid growth of *instituted* freedom here, than could have been done if the first million of inhabitants which our soil nourished, breaking up their homes, had returned to the Old World as crusaders against oppression? How fortunate that such myriads of Germans and Celts can come here and find not only the land welcoming them, but the homesteads and architecture of beneficent and tested institutions offering them protection! What if our past could be forgotten, and the millions of foreigners who press through our harbors toward the setting sun, were obliged to build their *liberties* as well as their log huts; to cultivate and organize the freedom they are to enjoy! How much less peace, how much less prosperity, would fall to their lot, than they now come in possession of, as inheritors of the principles and the consummate statesmanship of our Saxon builders in the past?

The mission of our land is still the path of organization, not aggressive propagandism or military interference. Let its influence be felt, in the lines of just and holy law, by process of construction through moral forces in favor of a higher national morality; by forcible protests against oppressive interference on the part of other nations in violation of the international code, but still with the dignity that shows the desire to keep the posture of peaceful friendship and practical instruction towards the European world.

Our responsibility to the oppressed of other lands is a deeper one than that of furnishing ammunition and supplies; it is the responsibility of faithfulness here to republican ideas, and of progress in the path suggested by the promptings of our history and the beckonings of Providence. Every noble institution we build up here is a more encouraging beacon to the struggling people of Europe than the fire-light of war. The striking off of each new fetter here resounds cheeringly through Europe. A musical tone travels much farther than a growl; and the effluence of a righteous victory of freedom on our shores will reach farther at last, and work more benefit for other races, than the sputter of our musketry in Trieste, and the roar of our floating batteries on the Danube. Let us not doubt that the wiping out of an oppressive statute in our code somehow makes the throne of Nicholas less firm. And all the prosperity, stability, and peace with which we invest the possession of freedom hasten the doom of foreign bondage, for they shed a light and a fragrance into the public sentiment that will guide the footsteps and revive the courage of the army of liberty in Europe, and they shame the lies that would brand republicanism as anarchy.

We have sent directly no ideas and no literature across the ocean to stir the popular heart to resistance, or to stimulate its aspirations; our influence has gone silently out from our institutions. The principle is as true with nations as in private life which Portia uttered, when she caught the gleam from home —

"How far that little candle throws its beams! So shines a good deed in a naughty world."

Despotism entrenches itself behind our errors and sins almost as securely as behind its own artillery. Let us make our Union a cluster of Christian Commonwealths, and the death-knell of Absolutism is struck by the decree that makes *character* the highest force in civilization.

And so the second lesson of our theme warns us and beseeches us, as patriots and as lovers of the world, to go on in the work of organization. Our fathers have left us a work to do. We are no spiritual children of theirs if we believe that all which is desirable, and can be made safely operative in society, has been embodied here; and plainly enough there are unfinished portions of their scheme which it is for our generation and those who come after us, to complete, out of reverence for their memory, adoration of the truth and love of mankind.

If there is a race within our borders for which there is no organization of liberty, but upon whom the architecture of the Saxon institutions frowns like the sullen masonry of forts and jails; to whom their security is the security of the dungeon; and for whom the strength of law is the strength of bolts and chains: how plain is the call upon those of our people whose hands can help them, to consider their case in the light and by the methods of a practical and sinewy wisdom !

How plain is the call upon us to give up as miserable, vapid, and boyish, all the declamation which overlooks the rooted strength, and is weak enough to treat it as an *idea* which denunciation and rhetoric can expunge; and to take hold of it as a problem of life, that may take generations perhaps to solve, but yet that must be solved, guided

by the fixed principle that there must come the
time when every human being who stands on
American soil shall have rights that are hedged by
friendly statutes, and a sacred freedom which the
whole spirit of society is pledged to maintain.

And in whatever way the spirit of social justice
can be made to enter more deeply into our
policy, or domesticate itself in new features of
our code without disruption of order, — in plans
of land reform, — in adjustments of the relations of labor, so that the laborer may be
more efficiently a man, — in the projection of
schemes for the safety and nurture of the perish-
ing classes, — we are called on cautiously to make
the experiment; and to show how far and with
what results the *forces of society* may shoot out
into regions that have hitherto been abandoned
to grim laws of competition and caprices of
private charity.

The grandeur and worth of our institutions
call on us, as the inheritors of them, to remem-
ber the conditions, and inhale the spirit by
which alone the most firmly founded organization can be upheld. It is a great thing that a
body has been given, so symmetrical and so
vigorous, for the shrine of freedom here; that
the organization of muscles and of nerves, of

Kossuth's power to establish there the institutions which the people love. Alas! if because
France has been cursed with a few mental
fiends, who would build up a *red republic*, we
are to look with complacency on the gambling
tyranny that dictates a despotic constitution from
the mouth of perjury, that steals by one trick of
universal suffrage the chance to crush the right of
representation and choke the press, that distributes
the functions of government among epaulettes,
and that graciously grants to the nations the right
and the blessing of unrestricted trade.

Where is the American spirit that should be
nurtured by our institutions, if, in the very light
of our history, we are to distrust the power of
the people to organize better institutions for themselves than the brain of a tyrant can devise?
Do you say that the path of revolution for
Europe is a perilous and shaded way? We
know it. But the last spirit to be fostered in the
American breast is that which would bring all
the perils that may beset the popular effort
for self-government into any comparison with
the quiet maintained by unscrupulous despotism.
Institutions like ours Europe may not be able
to establish, may not devise, may not desire; a
long and bloody storm may intervene between

the overthrow of oppression and the organization
of peace; but it is not for us to preach and
nourish hopeless distrust of the ability of popular
Europe, — if left for a generation, or for half a
century, in the experiment of liberty, — to correct
mistakes, to prune excesses, and to find the
preparation for republicanism which we so ear-
nestly talk about, but which will never be gained
by living under the shadow of absolute thrones.

And finally, we are warned by our history
not to distrust the capacity of the human race
to attain a social order upon the earth of a
higher stamp than any yet secured. It is *justice* which, thus far in human experience, has
been heaving the foundations of society, that
some of its principles may gain a solid place.
The great struggle has been to balance the
interests of the masses against the power of
the few, so that nature might be, in some
sense, a home for them, and existence a blessing. In the institution of such justice, at least
for the white races, our land stands preëminent,
far ahead of the nations that have gone before.
Two centuries ago it would have seemed im-
possible, Utopian, to the wisest statesman and
thinkers of the other world, to realize on a
scale such as this country now exhibits, such

a scheme of self-supporting, orderly and stable democracy. But there are dreams of men, yes, promises of a wisdom higher than man's, that this earth is yet to be the scene of organizations nobler than those of justice, — organizations of *love*. It is inspiring to think of some far-off centuries as destined to witness the birth, the progress, and the completion of such a blessing for our race. And, looking at our condition from the cruel feudal times, or from the level of a Patagonian degradation, such an organization of love upon the earth does not seem wholly a dream. And so this great value belongs to our history, that the philosophy of it helps our Christian hope. It makes prophecy seem more sober. It brings the rhetoric of Isaiah within the sympathy of common sense.

It is a summit from which the thinker may look off, like Moses from the mount, upon new and charming fields lying sweet in the smile of Heaven, where the armies of humanity — that have come up out of the bondage of despotism, and marched with sadness, but with courage, through the wastes and the want of the desert of selfishness, — shall find a home, shall build amid plenty, and enjoy in peace; and the nations, bound into solidarity of life despite their varieties, — as the globe, with all its latitudes and zones, its polar and tropic climes, its mountains and prairies, its streams and seas, is organized into one physical republic, — "shall beat their swords into ploughshares and their spears into pruning-hooks," and praise the Creator through a life of song, labor, and prayer.